# Contents

KU-711-093

# Being a TV Presenter

John Bilyard & Iris Howden

Published in association with The Basic Skills Agency

Hodder & Stoughton

A MEMBER OF THE HODDER HEADLINE GROUP

**Acknowledgements**

*Cover: Top of the Pops/The BBC*

*Photos: p 2 © David Cheskin/'PA' Photos; p 5 © Peter Jordan/'PA' Photos; p 8 © Jeff Spicer/Alpha; p 12 © Tim Ockenden/'PA' Photos; p 16 © Peter Aitchison/Alpha; p 20 © Mark Allan/Alpha.*

Every effort has been made to trace copyright holders of material reproduced in this book. Any rights not acknowledged will be acknowledged in subsequent printings if notice is given to the publisher.

Orders: please contact Bookpoint Ltd, 39 Milton Park, Abingdon, Oxon OX14 4TD. Telephone (44) 01235 400414, Fax: (44) 01235 400454. Lines are open from 9.00–6.00, Monday to Saturday, with a 24 hour message answering service. Email address: orders@bookpoint.co.uk

*British Library Cataloguing in Publication Data*
A catalogue record for this title is available from the British Library

ISBN 0 340 80068 2

First published 2001
Impression number    10 9 8 7 6 5 4 3 2 1
Year                           2007 2006 2005 2004 2003 2002 2001

Typeset by SX Composing DTP, Rayleigh, Essex.
Printed in Great Britain for Hodder & Stoughton Educational, a division of Hodder Headline Plc, 338 Euston Road, London NW1 3BH, by Redwood Books, Trowbridge, Wiltshire.

# 1   Jill Dando

The British public were shocked.
Popular TV presenter Jill Dando had been shot dead.
TV viewers loved Jill.
She had become part of their lives.
She was a friend they admired and trusted.
A familiar face on their TV screens.

Jill had all the qualities of a good TV presenter.
She was attractive.
She had a great personality.
A warm sense of humour.

Jill presented the BBC news.
She also fronted many other programmes.
People felt she almost came into their homes.
She had a special way of sharing things
with her viewers.
Viewers shared the sadness of tragic news items.
They shared Jill's enjoyment
on her holiday programmes.
They helped her and the police on *Crimewatch*.

Her death left a huge gap.

Jill Dando was a popular TV presenter.

# 2   The Job of the TV Presenter

Presenters are an important part of television.
They link the viewer to the TV programme.
They read the news.
They interview people.
They host talk and chat shows.
They ask the questions on quiz shows.
They bring sport into our living rooms.
They introduce the stars on variety shows.
They tell us about the weather.

We all have our favourite TV presenters.
And there are probably some we can't stand.
TV viewers are very quick to say what they think.
They email or write to the TV channels.

Does the weather girl have to giggle so much?
We don't like the sports presenter's moustache.
Can't he shave it off?
Please send me a signed photograph
of the business reporter.

Many TV presenters have their own fan clubs.
They receive millions of letters each year.
In many ways they are like film stars.

# 3   News Presenters

The news is an important part of television.
It keeps us in touch with the world.
It makes us think about important issues.
Many news programmes have two presenters.
Often they are a man and a woman.
Some people can follow a woman's voice
better than a man's.
For others a man's voice is easier.
A pair of presenters helps hold
the viewer's attention.
They can also react with each other.

A presenter's voice is very important.
If it is not attractive, people will switch off.
Most TV presenters have had voice training.
They have to pronounce difficult words
and foreign names.
But there is always an expert to help them.

News presenters must use the right tone of voice.
It must match the news they are reading.

Newsreaders, like Trevor McDonald, have to be
professional at all times.

One newsreader read the story
of a kitten trapped up a tree.
Someone called the fire brigade.
The firefighters came and rescued the kitten.
The old lady who owned the kitten was very pleased.
She invited the firefighters in for a cup of tea.
As they drove away they ran over the kitten.

At the end of the story the reader got a fit of the giggles.
Hundreds of animal lovers complained.
The presenter had reacted in the wrong way.

Before the news programmes, presenters rehearse.
But there is always the unexpected.
Things happen while the news is going out.
The death of someone famous or an election result.

Newsreaders have to react quickly.
They must never be fazed. They need nerves of steel.

Anna Ford was half-way through the news.
Suddenly there was a disturbance.
Some gay-rights protesters had got into the studio.
They chained themselves to Anna Ford's desk.

Anna stayed calm.
She explained to the viewers what was happening.
The protesters were removed.
Anna continued with the news.

# 4   Breakfast Television

For many years television didn't start
until late in the day.
Today breakfast television is with us.
Many people sit in front of the TV
with their cornflakes.
They check the latest news and weather.
They find out if there are problems on the roads.

The style of breakfast TV is different on each channel.
BBC breakfast television contains mostly news items.
The presenters wear smart, formal clothes.

*GMTV – Good Morning Television –*
on ITV is more upbeat.
The sets are bright and colourful.
It deals with light-hearted items.
The gossip from Hollywood.
What's happening in the soaps.

Channel 4's *The Big Breakfast* is very wacky.
It is more like a party than a news programme.
Johnny Vaughan and Denise van Outen
used to present it.
They used quick-fire humour and made fun of politics.

The presenters on *The Big Breakfast* are very relaxed.

Denise van Outen is a star in her own right.
A new word was used to describe Denise.
The word was 'ladette'.
It means a girl who acts in an upfront way.
Other ladette presenters are Zoë Ball and Sara Cox.

Denise says the life of a TV presenter
is not all glamour.
It's hard work.
*The Big Breakfast* goes out on Channel 4 at 7am.
The presenters have to get up 3.30am.
There are preparations for the programme
before it starts.
Denise says she found it hard.
Especially as her boyfriend works late.
He often doesn't get home until 3am!

*The Big Breakfast* is very popular with young people.
They like the style of the presenters.
They enjoy a laugh at the news.
They remember the jokes and tell them at school.
They like the fact that it's upbeat.

But it's good that there is something for all tastes.

# 5  Getting the Answers

The job of a TV interviewer is very hard.
Programmes like *Newsnight* and *Panorama*
try to bring out the truth.
This means some very tough interviewing.
But the interviewer mustn't go too far.
Guests have sometimes walked out.

Interviewers need to be very well prepared.
They have research assistants.
They find out all they can about the guest.
Then the interviewer works out the main questions.

But the interviewer doesn't know
how the guest will answer.
He or she must react quickly.
The interview has to be kept going.
Above all, interviewers must be fair.
They must try not to show their own points of view.

TV interviewers often have a background in law.
Watch a lawyer in court.
Then watch a TV interviewer at work.
You will see they are very similar.

# 6  Baring All

The talk show began life in America.
It's popular and cheap to produce.
Oprah Winfrey, Jerry Springer and Ricki Lake
are now well known in this country too.
The presenters expose people's private lives.
They bring the cheating husband and his wife
face to face.
Then the man's lover comes into the studio.
Tempers may become frayed.
Fists may fly.
The presenter tries to keep order.
And the public love it!
It's a bit like spying through a keyhole!
And the presenter is the one who makes it all happen.

Some presenters have been accused of cheating.
Have they used actors and not real people?
People's problems have seemed too far-fetched.
Like the long-distance lorry driver.
He had five wives and fifteen children.
The presenter brought all five wives into the studio.
They were soon fighting.
The lorry driver slipped away in the chaos.

Jerry Springer and Richard Branson have a pretend fight on the *Jerry Springer show*.

But talk-show hosts claim their guests are real people.
People are strange, they say.
There is no need to get them to pretend.

Kilroy is one of the most popular
British TV presenters.
He comes from a family of lawyers.
He practised as a lawyer himself
before he went into television.

Kilroy charms his guests.
They open up to him.
And we learn all about their secrets.

Trisha and Esther Rantzen are also popular.
ChildLine was set up following
one of Esther's programmes.
It helps children with any kind of problem.

Entertainment or bad taste?
Perhaps both.
But the talk show is with us to stay.

# 7 Helping the Police with Their Enquiries

*Crimewatch* made Jill Dando
and Nick Ross household names.
They became the link between the police and the public.
People may find it hard to contact the police.
But ringing *Crimewatch* is easier.
Jill and Nick were the faces of fair play.
Jill and Nick were faces you could trust.
It was easy to pick up the phone.

The programme also used police officers
as presenters.
They talked about stolen property
that had been recovered.
Or they gave details of crimes.
There is sometimes a barrier between
the police and the public.
*Crimewatch* helped to break it down.

Thousands of criminals have been caught
through *Crimewatch*.
A woman gave herself up
when she saw her picture on TV.
The police even arrested a suspect
while he was watching *Crimewatch*!

# 8   Quiz Show Presenters

Some people can't bear to miss
their favourite quiz show.
They are almost addicts.
It is usually the presenter who makes
the quiz show popular.

Les Dennis is a comedian.
He presents *Family Fortunes*.
Viewers like Les.
He makes the contestants laugh.
This is a good way of making them relax.

Angus Deayton has a dry sense of humour.
His long face rarely smiles.
Angus Deayton is also a comedian and actor.
He used to play Victor Meldrew's neighbour.
Angus hosts *Have I Got News for You*.
He and the team members have a laugh about politics.
They don't care what they say about famous people.
They get very close to libel.
They can also be very crude.
This is why the programme goes out after the
watershed at 9pm.

*They Think It's All Over* is a very funny sports quiz show.

Some quiz shows are just
for laughs rather than prizes.
Shows like *Shooting Stars*
and *They Think It's All Over.*
Nobody cares about the final score.
Everybody has had a good time.
Including the audience at home.

Nick Hancock is another comedian
who presents a quiz show.
*They Think It's All Over* is a sports quiz show.
Nick is very rude to his guests.
But he does it in a jokey way.
They don't take offence.
In fact, they give him as good as they get.

Nick Hancock was a teacher
before he went into television.
So were Chris Tarrant and Jim Bowen.
What makes ex-teachers good TV presenters?
Perhaps they are used to asking questions.
Or perhaps they just like being in charge!

Chris Tarrant used to be a children's TV presenter.
He now hosts *Who Wants to Be a Millionaire?*
The show is high in the ratings.

This is due to Chris's skill as a quizmaster.
He knows how to build up the tension.
Chris is quite serious.
But he supports the contestants.
He is truly sorry if they lose.
He is very different when he hosts *Tarrant on TV*.
On this programme everything is a riot!

Another serious quiz-show presenter is W. J. Stewart.
He presents *Fifteen to One*.
The questions on *Fifteen to One* are harder.
There are no really big prizes.
But hundreds of people apply to go on the show.

The most serious quiz presenter of all
is Anne Robinson.
She is best known for presenting *Watchdog*.
This is a programme about consumer issues.
Her quiz show, *The Weakest Link*,
is very popular.
The weakest member of the team
is voted out by the others.
Anne looks very strict
in her black-rimmed glasses.
She looks over them at the contestants.
'You should have known that,' she sneers.
When someone is knocked out she snaps, 'Goodbye.'

# 9  Presenting Variety Shows

'It's Friday and it's *Top of the Pops*!'
This programme is a must for pop-music lovers.
Young and old watch it.
It's noisy and colourful.
Everyone loves their favourite artist.
And everyone loves their favourite presenter.

Many *Top of the Pops* presenters were once DJs.
They know how to introduce a song.
They know how to stir up the audience.
And they know a lot about music.
Viewers know their voice.
They recognise them from pop magazines.

Sara Cox, Jamie Theakston, Jayne Middlemiss and
Richard Blackwood are some of today's presenters.
Sometimes the old-timers like Jimmy Savile
make a guest appearance!

The presenters on *Top of the Pops* are often DJs.

Matthew Kelly presents *Stars in Their Eyes*.
Contestants take off famous singers.
Matthew is very encouraging.
He builds the contestants up.
Viewers vote for the best performer.
Matthew has helped many performers.
They have gone on to become stars.

We all like a bit of romance.
*Blind Date* is a very popular programme.
It is presented by Cilla Black.
Cilla was a pop star in the 1960s.
Most couples don't get on too well
on their blind date.
Some find the right person.
But it's all good fun.
Cilla never lets things get too serious.

Dale Winton was always a bit of a joke.
Some people thought he had no talent.
But Dale was determined
to make it in showbusiness.
His shows were *Supermarket Sweep*
and *Pets Win Prizes*.
He was friendly and outgoing.
He brought out the best in people.
Dale now presents the National Lottery
and *The Other Half*.

# 10  Do I Need a Coat Today?

The British love to talk about the weather.
It's not surprising that we watch
the weather forecast on TV.
And we all have our favourite weather presenter.

Ulrika Jonsson began her career
as a weather presenter.
She had a sparkling personality.
She had sexy good looks.
She was once voted 'Rear of the Year.'
She went on to star in many other shows.

John Kettley had a song written about him.
He has many admirers.

Michael Fish once got the weather badly wrong.
He said there was no danger of storms and gales.
Next day Britain had its worst storm for years!
Michael still blushes when he thinks about it.

Weather presenters have to look smart.
They also have to train for many years.
They spend a lot of the day studying the weather.
Their five minutes on TV is only the tip of the iceberg!

# 11  Sports Presenters

There's nothing like it!
Standing on the terraces on a cold day.
Seeing the breath coming from your mouth.
Cheering on your favourite team.
Sport has caught the imagination of the nation.

For many years you went out
to a sports event to enjoy it.
Or you could listen on the radio.
Or read about it in the newspaper.
Television has changed all that.
Now you can enjoy sport
in the comfort of your own home.
Presenters tell us everything we need to know.
They lead us into the match.
They comment on action replays.
They interview the players and the fans.

Des Lynam is a popular sports presenter.
He brings humour into sport.
He recently switched from BBC to ITV.
He is one of the highest-paid sports presenters.

*Grandstand* is the BBC's showcase
sports programme.
It runs for over five and a half hours.
Saturday afternoon is the big time for sport.
Steve Rider introduces *Grandstand*.
He is a real enthusiast.
Steve holds the programme together.
He tells viewers which sports are going to feature.
Then he hands over to other presenters.
They introduce their favourite sports.
Most of them were once
famous sportspeople themselves.

Peter Scudamore was a famous jockey.
He introduces horse racing.
He captures the excitement of a big race.
He knows there is big money to be made in betting.
And big money to be lost.

Football, boxing, tennis and swimming –
*Grandstand* covers them all.
Snooker and darts are also popular.
And for each sport there is a presenter.
They have expert knowledge.
They make sure we enjoy their sport.
It's almost as if we were really there.

# 12  Learning from TV Presenters

Many TV programmes teach us new skills.
And the presenter becomes our friendly tutor.

Delia Smith, Gary Rhodes,
Jamie Oliver and Ainsley Harriott
are all expert cooks.
Through television they share their skills with us.
When the programme is over we can try for ourselves.

Gardening programmes such as *Ground Force*
have become very popular.
Alan Titchmarsh is an expert gardener.
He is helped by Charlie Dimmock and Tommy Walsh.
Charlie is best known for her auburn hair.
And for not wearing a bra!
She now presents her own programme.
It is called *Charlie's Garden Army*.
It gives people ideas for their own garden.
It pleases a lot of armchair gardeners, too!

Tommy Walsh is the bricklayer on *Ground Force*.
But he has also presented a fashion show!

Carol Smillie is a very popular presenter.
Like Ulrika Jonsson she was once voted
'Rear of the Year'.
Carol presents *Changing Rooms*.
It gives people's houses a makeover.
Sometimes they like what the team has done.
Sometimes they cry with disappointment.

Laurence Llewelyn-Bowen is one of the designers
in *Changing Rooms*.
He wears flashy clothes.
Not everyone likes his designs.
The programme has made him a star.
He now presents his own show.

Laurence works alongside Handy Andy.
Andy is the DIY expert.
He is very different from Laurence.
He is very down-to-earth.
Sometimes the two presenters disagree.
But they get the job done.

*Changing Rooms* has a big impact on viewers.
Many people have tried out
the ideas in their own home.

# 13  How to Become a TV Presenter

TV presenting is a tough career to get into.
There are not many courses.
The BBC has one.
Performing arts courses are very popular.
These can be a way into TV.
But at the end of a course
there is no guarantee of work.

Many TV presenters begin work as journalists.
It gets them used to meeting people.
It helps them master the English language.
Angela Rippon and Anna Ford
started as journalists.
Sometimes people start in radio.
Then they move across to TV.
Chris Evans started off as a radio DJ.

Those who succeed must be determined.
They must have staying power.
Good looks and personality are a must.
They must like people.
Confidence will get them a long way.

Top TV presenters earn very good money.
But it's tough at the top.
And there's always someone new
looking over your shoulder.

There are even virtual presenters like Ananova.
You can find them on the Web.
But the demand for human presenters continues.

In 2000, the BBC held a contest.
It was called 'BBC Talent'.
The idea was to find new young presenters.
Tests were held in major big cities in Britain.
Contestants had to talk about themselves.
Then they had to read a script.
Tapes were sent to London.
Area winners were chosen.
They went on to make screen tests
at the BBC TV Centre.

The BBC were looking for young people with spark.
They had to be confident all-rounders.
They could be asked to present
a whole range of programmes.
The BBC wanted to attract people
from all backgrounds.
Most of all they wanted to find fresh talent.
The young TV presenters of tomorrow.